Great Works Instructional Guides for **Literature**

THE VERY HUNGRY CATERPILLAR

A guide for the book by Eric Carle
Great Works Author: Brenda A. Van Dixhorn

SHELL EDUCATION

Publishing Credits

Robin Erickson, *Production Director;* Lee Aucoin, *Creative Director;*
Timothy J. Bradley, *Illustration Manager*; Emily R. Smith, M.A.Ed., *Editorial Director*; Amber Goff, *Editorial Assistant*; Don Tran, *Production Supervisor;*
Corinne Burton, M.A.Ed., *Publisher*

Image Credits

Susan Estelle Kwas (cover; pages 11–12); All other images from Shutterstock

Standards

© 2007 Teachers of English to Speakers of Other Languages, Inc. (TESOL)
© 2007 Board of Regents of the University of Wisconsin System. World-Class Instructional Design and Assessment (WIDA)
© Copyright 2010. National Governors Association Center for Best Practices and Council of Chief State School Officers.
All rights reserved.

Shell Education

5301 Oceanus Drive
Huntington Beach, CA 92649-1030
http://www.shelleducation.com

ISBN 978-1-4258-8972-2

© 2014 Shell Educational Publishing, Inc.

Table of contents

How to Use This Literature Guide

Today's standards demand rigor and relevance in the reading of complex texts. The units in this series guide teachers in a rich and deep exploration of worthwhile works of literature for classroom study. The most rigorous instruction can also be interesting and engaging!

Many current strategies for effective literacy instruction have been incorporated into these instructional guides for literature. Throughout the units, text-dependent questions are used to determine comprehension of the book as well as student interpretation of the vocabulary words. The books chosen for the series are complex and are exemplars of carefully crafted works of literature. Close reading is used throughout the units to guide students toward revisiting the text and using textual evidence to respond to prompts orally and in writing. Students must analyze the story elements in multiple assignments for each section of the book. All of these strategies work together to rigorously guide students through their study of literature.

The next few pages describe how to use this guide for a purposeful and meaningful literature study. Each section of this guide is set up in the same way to make it easier for you to implement the instruction in your classroom.

Theme Thoughts

The great works of literature used throughout this series have important themes that have been relevant to people for many years. Many of the themes will be discussed during the various sections of this instructional guide. However, it would also benefit students to have independent time to think about the key themes of the book.

Before students begin reading, have them complete the *Pre-Reading Theme Thoughts* (page 14). This graphic organizer will allow students to think about the themes outside the context of the story. They'll have the opportunity to evaluate statements based on important themes and defend their opinions. Be sure to keep students' papers for comparison to the *Post-Reading Theme Thoughts* (page 60). This graphic organizer is similar to the pre-reading activity. However, this time, students will be answering the questions from the point of view of one of the characters in the book. They have to think about how the character would feel about each statement and defend their thoughts. To conclude the activity, have students compare what they thought about the themes before they read the book to what the characters discovered during the story.

How to Use This Literature Guide (cont.)

Vocabulary

Each teacher reference vocabulary overview page has definitions and sentences about how key vocabulary words are used in the section. These words should be introduced and discussed with students. Students will use these words in different activities throughout the book.

On some of the vocabulary student pages, students are asked to answer text-related questions about vocabulary words from the sections. The following question stems will help you create your own vocabulary questions if you'd like to extend the discussion.

- How does this word describe _____'s character?
- How does this word connect to the problem in this story?
- How does this word help you understand the setting?
- Tell me how this word connects to the main idea of this story.
- What visual pictures does this word bring to your mind?
- Why do you think the author used this word?

At times, you may find that more work with the words will help students understand their meanings and importance. These quick vocabulary activities are a good way to further study the words.

- Students can play vocabulary concentration. Make one set of cards that has the words on them and another set with the definitions. Then, have students lay them out on the table and play concentration. The goal of the game is to match vocabulary words with their definitions. For early readers or English language learners, the two sets of cards could be the words and pictures of the words.

- Students can create word journal entries about the words. Students choose words they think are important and then describe why they think each word is important within the book. Early readers or English language learners could instead draw pictures about the words in a journal.

- Students can create puppets and use them to act out the vocabulary words from the stories. Students may also enjoy telling their own character-driven stories using vocabulary words from the original stories.

How to Use This Literature Guide *(cont.)*

Analyzing the Literature

After you have read each section with students, hold a small-group or whole-class discussion. Provided on the teacher reference page for each section are leveled questions. The questions are written at two levels of complexity to allow you to decide which questions best meet the needs of your students. The Level 1 questions are typically less abstract than the Level 2 questions. These questions are focused on the various story elements, such as character, setting, and plot. Be sure to add further questions as your students discuss what they've read. For each question, a few key points are provided for your reference as you discuss the book with students.

Reader Response

In today's classrooms, there are often great readers who are below average writers. So much time and energy is spent in classrooms getting students to read on grade level that little time is left to focus on writing skills. To help teachers include more writing in their daily literacy instruction, each section of this guide has a literature-based reader response prompt. Each of the three genres of writing is used in the reader responses within this guide: narrative, informative/explanatory, and opinion. Before students write, you may want to allow them time to draw pictures related to the topic. Book-themed writing paper is provided on page 70 if your students need more space to write.

Guided Close Reading

Within the first four sections of this guide, it is suggested that you closely reread a portion of the text with your students. The sections to be reread are described by location within the story since there are no page numbers in this book. After rereading the section, there are a few text-dependent questions to be answered by students. Working space has been provided to help students prepare for the group discussion. They should record their thoughts and ideas on the activity page and refer to it during your discussion. Rather than just taking notes, you may want to require students to write complete responses to the questions before discussing them with you.

Encourage students to read one question at a time and then go back to the text and discover the answer. Work with students to ensure that they use the text to determine their answers rather than making unsupported inferences. Suggested answers are provided in the answer key.

How to Use This Literature Guide (cont.)

Guided Close Reading (cont.)

The generic open-ended stems below can be used to write your own text-dependent questions if you would like to give students more practice.

- What words in the story support . . . ?
- What text helps you understand . . . ?
- Use the book to tell why _____ happens.
- Based on the events in the story, . . . ?
- Show me the part in the text that supports . . . .
- Use the text to tell why . . . .

Making Connections

The activities in this section help students make cross-curricular connections to mathematics, science, social studies, fine arts, or other curricular areas. These activities require higher-order thinking skills from students but also allow for creative thinking.

Language Learning

A special section has been set aside to connect the literature to language conventions. Through these activities, students will have opportunities to practice the conventions of standard English grammar, usage, capitalization, and punctuation.

Story Elements

It is important to spend time discussing what the common story elements are in literature. Understanding the characters, setting, plot, and theme can increase students' comprehension and appreciation of the story. If teachers begin discussing these elements in early childhood, students will more likely internalize the concepts and look for the elements in their independent reading. Another very important reason for focusing on the story elements is that students will be better writers if they think about how the stories they read are constructed.

In the story elements activities, students are asked to create work related to the characters, setting, or plot. Consider having students complete only one of these activities. If you give students a choice on this assignment, each student can decide to complete the activity that most appeals to him or her. Different intelligences are used so that the activities are diverse and interesting to all students.

How to Use This Literature Guide (cont.)

Culminating Activity

At the end of this instructional guide is a creative culminating activity that allows students the opportunity to share what they've learned from reading the book. This activity is open ended so that students can push themselves to create their own great works within your language arts classroom.

Comprehension Assessment

The questions in this section require students to think about the book they've read as well as the words that were used in the book. Some questions are tied to quotations from the book to engage students and require them to think about the text as they answer the questions.

Response to Literature

Finally, students are asked to respond to the literature by drawing pictures and writing about the characters and stories. A suggested rubric is provided for teacher reference.

Correlation to the Standards

Shell Education is committed to producing educational materials that are research and standards based. As part of this effort, we have correlated all of our products to the academic standards of all 50 states, the District of Columbia, the Department of Defense Dependents Schools, and all Canadian provinces.

Purpose and Intent of Standards

Standards are designed to focus instruction and guide adoption of curricula. Standards are statements that describe the criteria necessary for students to meet specific academic goals. They define the knowledge, skills, and content students should acquire at each level. Standards are also used to develop standardized tests to evaluate students' academic progress. Teachers are required to demonstrate how their lessons meet standards. Standards are used in the development of all of our products, so educators can be assured they meet high academic standards.

How to Find Standards Correlations

To print a customized correlation report of this product for your state, visit our website at http://www.shelleducation.com and follow the online directions. If you require assistance in printing correlation reports, please contact our Customer Service Department at 1-877-777-3450.

correlation to the Standards (cont.)

Standards correlation chart

The lessons in this book were written to support the Common Core College and Career Readiness Anchor Standards. The following chart indicates which lessons address the anchor standards.

Common Core College and Career Readiness Anchor Standard	Section
CCSS.ELA-Literacy.CCRA.R.1—Read closely to determine what the text says explicitly and to make logical inferences from it; cite specific textual evidence when writing or speaking to support conclusions drawn from the text.	Guided Close Reading Sections 1–4; Making Connections Sections 3, 5
CCSS.ELA-Literacy.CCRA.R.2—Determine central ideas or themes of a text and analyze their development; summarize the key supporting details and ideas.	Analyzing the Literature Sections 1–5; Guided Close Reading Sections 1–4; Post-Reading Theme Thoughts
CCSS.ELA-Literacy.CCRA.R.3—Analyze how and why individuals, events, or ideas develop and interact over the course of a text.	Analyzing the Literature Sections 1–5; Guided Close Reading Sections 1–4; Story Elements Sections 1, 4
CCSS.ELA-Literacy.CCRA.R.8—Delineate and evaluate the argument and specific claims in a text, including the validity of the reasoning as well as the relevance and sufficiency of the evidence.	Analyzing the Literature Sections 1–5; Guided Close Reading Sections 1–4
CCSS.ELA-Literacy.CCRA.R.9— Analyze how two or more texts address similar themes or topics in order to build knowledge or to compare the approaches the authors take.	Entire Unit
CCSS.ELA-Literacy.CCRA.W.1—Write arguments to support claims in an analysis of substantive topics or texts using valid reasoning and relevant and sufficient evidence.	Reader Response Section 3; Post-Reading Response to Literature
CCSS.ELA-Literacy.CCRA.W.2—Write informative/explanatory texts to examine and convey complex ideas and information clearly and accurately through the effective selection, organization, and analysis of content.	Reader Response Sections 2, 4
CCSS.ELA-Literacy.CCRA.W.3—Write narratives to develop real or imagined experiences or events using effective technique, well-chosen details and well-structured event sequences.	Reader Response Sections 1, 5; Story Elements Section 3; Making Connections Section 5
CCSS.ELA-Literacy.CCRA.W.4—Produce clear and coherent writing in which the development, organization, and style are appropriate to task, purpose, and audience.	Reader Response Sections 1–5; Language Learning Sections 1, 5; Story Elements Sections 1–2; Post-Reading Response to Literature

correlation to the Standards (cont.)

Standards correlation chart (cont.)

Common Core College and Career Readiness Anchor Standard	Section
CCSS.ELA-Literacy.CCRA.SL.1—Prepare for and participate effectively in a range of conversations and collaborations with diverse partners, building on others' ideas and expressing their own clearly and persuasively	Analyzing the Literature Sections 1–5; Culminating Activity
CCSS.ELA-Literacy.CCRA.L.1—Demonstrate command of the conventions of standard English grammar and usage when writing or speaking.	Analyzing the Literature Sections 1–5; Language Learning Sections 1, 3–5
CCSS.ELA-Literacy.CCRA.L.2—Demonstrate command of the conventions of standard English capitalization, punctuation, and spelling when writing.	Language Learning Section 2
CCSS.ELA-Literacy.CCRA.L.4—Determine or clarify the meaning of unknown and multiple-meaning words and phrases by using context clues, analyzing meaningful word parts, and consulting general and specialized reference materials, as appropriate.	Vocabulary Sections 1–5
CCSS.ELA-Literacy.CCRA.L.5—Demonstrate understanding of figurative language, word relationships, and nuances in word meanings.	Vocabulary Sections 1–5
CCSS.ELA-Literacy.CCRA.L.6—Acquire and use accurately a range of general academic and domain-specific words and phrases sufficient for reading, writing, speaking, and listening at the college and career readiness level; demonstrate independence in gathering vocabulary knowledge when encountering an unknown term important to comprehension or expression.	Vocabulary Sections 1–5

TESOL and WIDA Standards

The lessons in this book promote English language development for English language learners. The following TESOL and WIDA English Language Development Standards are addressed through the activities in this book:

- **Standard 1:** English language learners communicate for social and instructional purposes within the school setting.

- **Standard 2:** English language learners communicate information, ideas and concepts necessary for academic success in the content area of language arts.

About the Author—Eric Carle

The name Eric Carle brings to mind many favorite children's books. Carle however was not always a children's author and illustrator. Before writing and illustrating children's books, Eric Carle worked as a graphic designer for the *New York Times* and was an art director at an advertising agency. A phone call and invitation from Bill Martin Jr. to illustrate the book *Brown Bear, Brown Bear, What Do You See?* started the career for which Carle is most well known.

Carle was born in 1929 in Syracuse, New York. Six years later, his family moved to Germany where he received his education and graduated from art school. Carle had many happy memories from his early youth, and in 1952 he realized his dream of returning to the United States.

The artwork of Eric Carle is distinct. He uses hand-painted papers to create layered collages. The books Carle creates present children with cheerful colors and interesting text that help them learn about the world around them.

Eric Carle has earned many awards and honors for his books. To learn more about this author and view a video of him reading *The Very Hungry Caterpillar*, visit his website at **http://www.eric-carle.com**.

Possible Texts for Text Comparisons

Eric Carle has more than 40 books in print. Several of his books are about insects. *The Grouchy Ladybug, The Very Busy Spider, The Very Quiet Cricket, The Very Lonely Firefly*, and *The Very Clumsy Click Beetle* may also be used for enriching text comparisons.

Book Summary of *The Very Hungry Caterpillar*

An unseen butterfly lays an egg on a leaf. *The Very Hungry Caterpillar* begins by showing this egg in the moonlight. When the sun rises, the egg hatches and out emerges a very hungry caterpillar. Eric Carle brings the reader along as the tiny caterpillar grows into a large caterpillar that builds a cocoon and eventually becomes a butterfly. An element of fantasy is added to this life cycle story through what the caterpillar eats. Rather than eating leaves as most caterpillars do, the very hungry caterpillar devours a wide assortment of foods that children also love to eat. Join the very hungry caterpillar on a journey through the days of the week as he attempts to quench his appetite and transform into a beautiful butterfly.

Cross-Curricular Connection

This book can be used to teach science life cycles, math counting and calendar concepts, health food groups, and social studies hopes and dreams. If you would like to give your students the opportunity to observe the life cycle of a butterfly, visit the Insect Lore website at **http://www.insectlore.com/** to order eggs and materials.

Possible Texts for Text Sets

- Ehlert, Lois. *Waiting for Wings*. HMH Books for Young Readers, 2001.
- Frost, Helen. *Monarch and Milkweed*. Atheneum Books for Young Readers, 2008.
- Marsh, Laura. *National Geographic Readers: Caterpillar to Butterfly*. National Geographic Children's Books, 2012.
- Martin, Bill Jr. *Ten Little Caterpillars*. Beach Lane Books, 2011.
- Flatharta, Antoine Ò. *Hurry and the Monarch*. Random House Children's Books, 2013.
- Ryder, Joanne. *Where Butterflies Grow*. Puffin, 1996.

or

- Berenstain, Stan and Jan Berenstain. *The Berenstain Bears and Too Much Junk Food*. Random House Books for Young Readers, 1985.
- Green, Emily K. *Healthy Eating*. Scholastic Library Publishing, 2011.
- Mitchell, Melanie. *Eating Well*. Lerner Classroom, 2006.
- Rabe, Tish. *Oh the Things You Can Do That Are Good for You!: All About Staying Healthy*. Random House Books for Young Readers, 2001.

  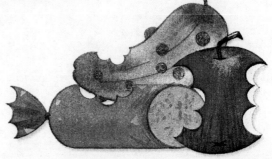

How to Read the Book

Each section of this instructional guide contains lessons and activities to help students gain an understanding of the story and related vocabulary in a variety of ways. A summary of each section is given below to be used as a guide each time you share this book with your class.

Section 1: Meet the Caterpillar

This section focuses on the way the caterpillar is described in the book. Many of the vocabulary words in this section are adjectives that describe the caterpillar throughout the story. Reading about the caterpillar and what he is like provides a good overview of the book.

Section 2: Watch the Caterpillar Change

This section has a science focus. As you read through the book this time, look at the steps involved to change from an egg to a beautiful butterfly. The vocabulary for this section focuses on scientific terms associated with the metamorphosis that occurs in the life cycle of a butterfly.

Section 3: Math Concepts with the Caterpillar

This section looks at the numbers in the book. Days of the week and size terms are introduced. As you read the book through, help children to see the sequence in the story. The vocabulary words highlighted for this section will help children gain an understanding of size, sequence, and position.

Section 4: What Should the Caterpillar Eat?

This section gives students an opportunity to learn about specific foods and think about healthy eating choices. While most of the foods the caterpillar eats are good, the amounts he eats are not healthy. This section allows children to evaluate the types and amounts of food necessary for a healthy diet.

Section 5: What Will Happen to the Caterpillar?

This section is a chance to explore, dream, and imagine what will happen next in the life of the butterfly. As you read the book to your students again, allow them to express their thoughts and ideas for the butterfly as well as dreams for their own lives. There is no guided close reading activity in this section.

Name _____

Pre-Reading Theme Thoughts

Directions: Read each statement. Draw a picture of a happy face or a sad face. The face should show how you feel about the statement. Then, use words to say why you feel this way.

Statement	How Do You Feel? 😊 ☹	Why Do You Feel That Way?
A character can change a lot between the beginning of a story and the end.		
A caterpillar stays very busy.		
It is important to make good food choices.		
It takes a lot of work to become a butterfly.		

#40008—Instructional Guide: The Very Hungry Caterpillar

Vocabulary Overview

Key words and phrases from this section are provided below with definitions and sentences about how the words are used in the story. Introduce and discuss these important vocabulary words with the students. If you think these words or other words in the story warrant more time devoted to them, there are suggestions in the introduction for other vocabulary activities (page 5).

Word	Definition	Sentence about Text
little	very small	There is a **little** egg on a leaf.
egg	round or oval thing from which something is born	The **egg** hatches into a caterpillar.
lay	to rest on an object	The little egg **lay** on a leaf.
tiny	below average size	When it hatches from the egg, the caterpillar is **tiny**.
hungry	a desire to eat food	The **hungry** caterpillar searches for food.
caterpillar	the wormlike larva of a butterfly or moth	A **caterpillar** is the main character of this book.
big	larger than average size	After he has eaten, the caterpillar is quite **big**.
fat	being a relatively large distance around	The caterpillar's stomach is so full he is described as being **fat**.
beautiful	pleasing to see	A **beautiful** butterfly hatches from the cocoon.
butterfly	an insect with a slender body, antennae, and colorful wings	The **butterfly** has colorful wings.

Name _____

Vocabulary Activity

Directions: Choose at least two words from the story. Draw a picture that shows what these words mean. Label your picture.

Words from the Story

little	egg	lay	tiny	hungry
caterpillar	big	fat	beautiful	butterfly

Directions: Answer this question.

1. What things besides a butterfly can be described as **beautiful**?

_____

_____

_____

Analyzing the Literature

Provided below are discussion questions you can use in small groups, with the whole class, or for written assignments. Each question is written at two levels so you can choose the right question for each group of students. For each question, a few key points are provided for your reference as you discuss the book with students.

Story Element	Level 1	Level 2	Key Discussion Points
Setting	Where do you think this story takes place?	In what season is this story most likely to occur?	The egg is seen in the light of the moon and hatches when the sun comes up, so the story takes place outdoors. Because butterflies need warm weather to complete their life cycle this story happens in the summer.
Plot	What does the caterpillar eat in the story?	What do caterpillars really eat?	The very hungry caterpillar eats a variety of fruits, sweets, and other foods. In reality, caterpillars eat mostly leaves, just as the caterpillar does before building his cocoon.
Character	Describe the main character in this story.	How does the main character change throughout the book?	We are first introduced to an egg, which then hatches into a caterpillar that finally changes into a butterfly. During the story the main character changes in form, size, color, and level of activity.
Plot	Could this story really happen? Why do you think that?	What parts of this story seem true and which parts seem fictional?	The life cycle of a butterfly is accurately described in this story. The food devoured by the caterpillar adds an element of fantasy.

Name _____

Reader Response

Think

Think about a time when you were really hungry. What types of food did you eat?

Narrative Writing Prompt

Tell about a time when you ate many different types of foods. What did you eat? How did you feel afterwards?

_____

- - - - - - - - - - - - - - - - - -

_____

- - - - - - - - - - - - - - - - - -

_____

- - - - - - - - - - - - - - - - - -

_____

- - - - - - - - - - - - - - - - - -

_____

- - - - - - - - - - - - - - - - - -

_____

- - - - - - - - - - - - - - - - - -

_____

- - - - - - - - - - - - - - - - - -

_____

Name _____

Guided close Reading

Closely reread the first and second pages of text from the story.

Directions: Think about these questions. In the chart, write ideas or draw pictures as you think. Be ready to share your answers.

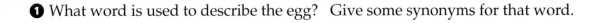

❶ What word is used to describe the egg? Give some synonyms for that word.

❷ What words are used to describe the caterpillar? What other words would you use to describe the caterpillar?

❸ Describe how the pictures help you understand the mood of these first few pages.

Name _____

Making connections—
Make Your own caterpillar!

Directions: Follow the directions to create your own caterpillar.

Materials

- white paper
- pencil
- crayons/markers

Directions

1. Draw a circle on the right side of your paper. This is your caterpillar's head.

2. Add two eyes, one nose, and two antennae to your circle. Draw a cute mouth, also.

3. Draw several ovals to the left of the head that connect to each other. You can make the caterpillar's body as long as you like.

4. Draw legs on your caterpillar.

5. Make your caterpillar colorful.

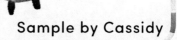

Sample by Cassidy

Name _____

Language Learning—Adjectives

happy

small

long

striped

curvy

hungry

The words surrounding the picture of the caterpillar are adjectives. Adjectives are words that describe people, places, or things.

Directions: Draw a person, a place, or a thing in each column. Below each drawing write at least two adjectives to describe your person, place, or thing.

Person	Place	Thing

Name _____

Story Elements—Setting

Directions: Where do you think this story takes place? Create a map showing where you think the caterpillar goes during this story. Be sure to label your map.

 #40008—Instructional Guide: The Very Hungry Caterpillar

Name _____

Story Elements—Plot

Directions: The caterpillar goes through many changes in this story. Create a cartoon to show what he might be thinking at the beginning, middle, and end of the story.

Vocabulary Overview

Key words and phrases from this section are provided below with definitions and sentences about how the words are used in the story. Introduce and discuss these important vocabulary words with the students. If you think these words or other words in the story warrant more time devoted to them, there are suggestions in the introduction for other vocabulary activities (page 5).

Word	Definition	Sentence about Text
egg	oval thing from which something is born	An adult butterfly lays an **egg** on a leaf.
hatch	emerge from an egg	When it is ready, a caterpillar **hatches** from the egg.
caterpillar	the wormlike larva of a butterfly or moth	The job of a **caterpillar** is to eat and grow.
larva	another name for a butterfly caterpillar	Another name for this story could be *The Very Hungry Larva*!
chrysalis	the place where a caterpillar changes into a butterfly	The caterpillar stays in the **chrysalis** and becomes a butterfly.
cocoon	a silky covering for a caterpillar	The caterpillar makes himself a **cocoon**.
butterfly	an insect with a slender body, antennae, and colorful wings	The **butterfly** has many beautiful colors.
emerge	come into view	A butterfly **emerges** from the chrysalis.
metamorphosis	to change in form	*The Very Hungry Caterpillar* is a story about **metamorphosis**.

Name _____

Vocabulary Activity

Directions: Draw a line to complete each sentence.

Beginnings of Sentences	Endings of Sentences
The small egg	hatches from an egg.
In the moonlight	called a cocoon.
The caterpillar	hatches when it's ready.
The caterpillar builds a small house	a small egg is on a leaf.
When he emerges from the cocoon,	he is a beautiful butterfly!

Directions: Answer this question.

1. What is another name for **larva**?

_____

_____

_____

Analyzing the Literature

Provided below are discussion questions you can use in small groups, with the whole class, or for written assignments. Each question is written at two levels so you can choose the right question for each group of students. For each question, a few key points are provided for your reference as you discuss the book with students.

Story Element	Level 1	Level 2	Key Discussion Points
Character	How does the character change in the story?	How do you think the caterpillar feels about the changes it makes?	This story shares the life cycle of a butterfly and the metamorphosis that takes place from egg to caterpillar to cocoon and finally to a butterfly. Encourage students to make inferences about how the caterpillar feels.
Setting	Why is the egg lying on a leaf?	How would this story be different if the egg was lying in the grass?	When caterpillars emerge from eggs, they want to eat. Adult butterflies lay their eggs on leaves that the caterpillars will eat.
Plot	What does the caterpillar do his first week as a caterpillar?	How long do you think it takes the caterpillar to change from an egg to a butterfly?	The caterpillar in this story spends one full week eating. Then it builds a cocoon and spends two weeks inside it before emerging as a butterfly.

Name _____

Reader Response

Think

Think about something in nature that changes. Why does it change?

Informative/Explanatory Writing Prompt

Describe something in nature that changes. Be sure to tell what it looks like before and after the change. Use lots of adjectives.

_____

- -

_____

- -

_____

- -

_____

- -

_____

- -

_____

- -

_____

Name _____

Guided close Reading

Closely reread the last three pages of the story.

Directions: Think about these questions. In the chart, write ideas or draw pictures as you think. Be ready to share your answers.

---

❶ Use words from the book to describe the caterpillar after eating all week.

---

❷ Based on the text, what do you know about the cocoon?

---

❸ What words in the story help you understand how long the caterpillar is in the cocoon?

Name _____

Making connections—Life Cycle

Directions: *The Very Hungry Caterpillar* tells about the life cycle of a butterfly.

1. Cut out the pictures below.

2. Attach them to your paper in the correct order.

3. Reorder these words to label the life cycle of the butterfly: cocoon, butterfly, caterpillar, and egg.

1.	2.	3.	4.

_____ _____ _____ _____

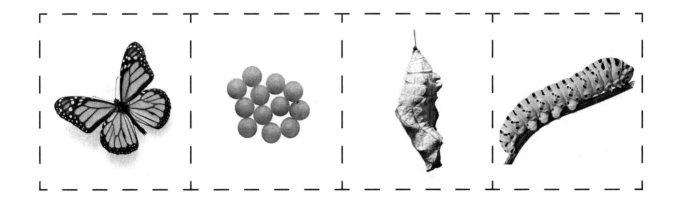

Name _____

Language Learning—Sentences

Directions: Think about the two parts of the character in this story: the caterpillar and the butterfly. How are they the same and how are they different? Write three sentences. Be sure to use capital letters and periods in your sentences.

_____

- -
_____

- -
_____

- -
_____

- -
_____

- -
_____

- -
_____

- -
_____

- -
_____

- -
_____

Name _____

Watch the caterpillar change

Story Elements—character

Directions: How would you change the caterpillar? Draw your own caterpillar that looks different from the one in the book. Tell a friend about your changed caterpillar.

© Shell Education   #40008—Instructional Guide: The Very Hungry Caterpillar   31

Name _____

Story Elements—Plot

Directions: Change the plot of this story. Pretend it is called *The Very Hungry Child*. Make a list of seven different foods you would eat if you were very hungry.

1. _____

2. _____

3. _____

4. _____

5. _____

6. _____

7. _____

Math concepts with the caterpillar
Vocabulary Overview

Key words and phrases from this section are provided below with definitions and sentences about how the words are used in the story. Introduce and discuss these important vocabulary words with the students. If you think these words or other words in the story warrant more time devoted to them, there are suggestions in the introduction for other vocabulary activities (page 5).

Word	Definition	Sentence about Text
started	began an activity	The caterpillar is hungry so he **starts** looking for food.
through	in and out of	The hungry caterpillar eats **through** a lot of food.
still	not changing	Even though he eats a lot of food, the caterpillar is **still** hungry.
piece	a section or part of something larger	The caterpillar eats through a **piece** of pie.
slice	a thin, flat piece cut off an object	The caterpillar finds **slices** of cheese, salami, and watermelon.
next	immediately following in time	The **next** day of the week is Sunday.
again	when something happens more than once	The egg hatches on Sunday and after a week passes it is Sunday **again**.
after	later in time	The caterpillar feels better **after** eating the leaf.

Name _____

Vocabulary Activity

Directions: Each of these sentences contains a word from the story. Cut apart these sentence strips. Put the sentences in order based on the events in the story.

He eats **through** a leaf and feels better.

He eats **through** three plums.

He **starts** to look for food.

The **next** day is Sunday **again**.

He eats through one **slice** of salami.

On Saturday he eats through one **piece** of chocolate cake.

Math concepts with the caterpillar
Analyzing the Literature

Provided below are discussion questions you can use in small groups, with the whole class, or for written assignments. Each question is written at two levels so you can choose the right question for each group of students. For each question, a few key points are provided for your reference as you discuss the book with the students.

Story Element	Level 1	Level 2	Key Discussion Points
Character	What is the caterpillar like at the start of the story?	Describe what might have happened just before the story started.	The egg did not get to the leaf by itself. Before this story ever started another egg changed to a caterpillar and then a butterfly. It was that butterfly that laid the tiny egg on the leaf.
Plot	Why is it not a good idea for the caterpillar to eat all the food he does?	Tell about a time when you ate too much food.	It probably is not a good idea for the caterpillar to eat so much food because he gets a stomachache. Allow students to share their experiences about not feeling well after eating too much food.
Plot	What is another way the caterpillar could have eaten the foods?	How long do you think it took the caterpillar to eat through all of the food?	Rather than eating through a piece of food, the caterpillar could nibble off a small portion. Considering the size of a caterpillar and the size of the foods he eats through, it probably takes a large part of the day to get through the food.
Setting	Where could you find the foods the caterpillar eats?	Where do you think the caterpillar finds all of the foods he eats?	Students can have fun imagining places where a caterpillar could have found such a wide variety of foods. Allow children to share places they find different foods such as their lunch boxes, the school cafeteria, the grocery store, a refrigerator, or a picnic basket.

Name _____

Reader Response

Think

This book
has counting
and days of
the week in
it. Both of
these are
math topics.

Opinion Writing Prompt

What is the best type of
math to do? Pick one
type of math problem and
describe why it's the best.

_____

- -

_____

_____

- -

_____

- -

_____

- -

_____

- -

_____

Name _____

Guided close Reading

Closely reread the story starting with him looking for food. Stop when he has a stomachache.

Directions: Think about these questions. In the chart, write ideas or draw pictures as you think. Be ready to share your answers.

❶ How does the book show that the caterpillar's hunger is growing throughout the week?

❷ Use the text and pictures to compare and contrast what the caterpillar eats Monday through Friday compared to what he eats on Saturday.

❸ What words tell about how the caterpillar feels after eating?

Name _____

Making Connections—
How Much Does He Eat?

Directions: The hungry caterpillar eats his way through the week. In the chart below, draw small pictures of the fruit he eats. Then tell how many pieces he eats of each fruit.

Day of the Week	Fruit the Caterpillar Eats	How Many Pieces?
Monday		
Tuesday		
Wednesday		
Thursday		
Friday		
Total Pieces of Fruit the Caterpillar Eats = _____		

Name _____

Language Learning—Plural Nouns

Directions: Fill in the blank for each sentence. Write a verb that matches each noun.

1. The caterpillar **eats** an apple.

_____

– – – – – – – – –

Caterpillars _____ apples.
(eat *or* eats)

• •

2. Caterpillars **like** to eat fruit.

_____

– – – – – – – – –

The caterpillar _____ to eat fruit.
(like *or* likes)

• •

3. The caterpillar **turns** into a butterfly.

_____

– – – – – – – – –

Caterpillars _____ into butterflies.
(turn *or* turns)

Name _____

Story Elements—Plot

Materials

- 3" x 5" card
- crayons or pencils

Directions

1. Look back at the book.

2. Think about each of the foods the caterpillar eats in the story.

3. Pick your favorite food from the story.

4. Draw a picture of your favorite food on a 3" x 5" card.

5. Work with your classmates to create a class graph of your cards.

6. Which food is the class's favorite?

   _____

   _ _ _ _ _ _ _ _ _ _ _ _ _ _ _ _ _ _

   _____

7. Which food is the class's least favorite?

   _____

   _ _ _ _ _ _ _ _ _ _ _ _ _ _ _ _ _ _

   _____

Story Elements—Setting

Directions: Pretend you are the butterfly. Write a note to tell the caterpillar what he will see and do when he pops out of the egg.

Dear Caterpillar,

_____

_____

_____

_____

_____

_____

_____

_____

From,

Butterfly

Vocabulary Overview

Key words and phrases from this section are provided below with definitions and sentences about how the words are used in the story. Introduce and discuss these important vocabulary words with the students. If you think these words or other words in the story warrant more time devoted to them, there are suggestions in the introduction for other vocabulary activities (page 5).

Word	Definition	Sentence about Text
plums	sweet fruit that has smooth skin and hard pits	The caterpillar eats through plums on Wednesday.
Swiss cheese	cheese from Switzerland made with many holes	He eats through a slice of Swiss cheese.
salami	seasoned hard sausage	On Saturday, the caterpillar eats through a slice of salami.
cherry pie	a pie filled with cooked cherries	The caterpillar enjoys a piece of cherry pie, as well.
sausage	seasoned meat inside a casing	The caterpillar tries eating sausage.
slice	a thin, flat piece cut off an object	The caterpillar finds slices of food to eat.
piece	a section or part of something larger	The caterpillar eats through a piece of cake.
through	in and out of	The caterpillar eats through many pieces of fruit.

Vocabulary Activity

Directions: Complete each sentence below with one of the vocabulary words listed here.

Words from the Story

plums	Swiss cheese	salami	cherry pie
sausage	slice	piece	through

1. On Sunday he eats through a _____
   of Swiss cheese.

2. The caterpillar eats through three _____.

3. He also eats through a piece of _____.

Directions: Answer this question.

4. What foods does the caterpillar eat **through**?

_____

_____

_____

_____

Analyzing the Literature

Provided below are discussion questions you can use in small groups, with the whole class, or for written assignments. Each question is written at two levels so you can choose the right question for each group of students. For each question, a few key points are provided for your reference as you discuss the book with the students.

Story Element	Level 1	Level 2	Key Discussion Points
Plot	What do you think the caterpillar's favorite foods are?	Discuss the foods you eat throughout the day.	The caterpillar's favorite foods may be fruits since he eats so many of them. This can be open to children's interpretations. Give children an opportunity to discuss types and amount of food they eat daily.
Setting	Which foods eaten by the caterpillar grow on trees and which are made or purchased in a store?	Tell what you know about the foods in the story.	The caterpillar eats many fruits that come directly from plants. Discuss how these plants grow and are harvested. Help children to identify the foods that are baked or processed.
Character	Why do you think the caterpillar eats so many different foods?	Explain why you think the caterpillar makes wise or unwise decisions about what he eats.	There can be many reasons the caterpillar eats such a wide variety of foods. During the week, the caterpillar makes healthy choices, but on Saturday, he eats many foods that are not as healthy, resulting in a stomachache.
Plot	Why does the caterpillar have a stomachache Saturday night?	What should the caterpillar have eaten to avoid getting a stomachache?	The caterpillar has a stomachache from the food he eats during the day. It could be because of the types of foods he eats or the amounts. Children will have different ideas about what would have been healthier for the caterpillar.

Name _____

Reader Response

Think

Think about the healthiest foods you eat. How do these foods help your body?

Informative/Explanatory Writing Prompt

Describe how healthy foods help you grow and stay healthy.

_____

_____

_____

_____

_____

_____

_____

_____

_____

_____

_____

Name _____

Guided close Reading

Closely reread the "Saturday" page as well as the following page where the caterpillar eats a leaf.

Directions: Think about these questions. In the chart, write ideas or draw pictures as you think. Be ready to share your answers.

❶ What words in the story tell you that eating all that food is not a good idea?

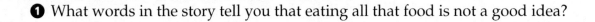

❷ Based on the text and picture, how many kinds of foods does the caterpillar eat on Saturday?

❸ Use words from the text to describe what the caterpillar does to recover from his stomachache.

Name _____

Making connections— Different Types of Foods

Directions: The tiny caterpillar eats many foods as he grows. Cut out the pictures of the foods. Sort the pictures into four groups: **Fruit/Vegetable**, **Dairy**, **Meat (protein)**, and **Empty Calories**.

Name _____

Language Learning—
Alphabetical Order

Directions: Here are some of the yummy foods the caterpillar eats. Rewrite the list of foods below in alphabetical order.

oranges	strawberries	apple
leaf	watermelon	ice-cream cone

1. _____

2. _____

3. _____

4. _____

5. _____

6. _____

Name _____

Story Elements—characters

Directions: Use the T-chart below. Add words to each side to show what you think the caterpillar might think and feel when he is each size.

Name _____

Story Elements—Setting

Directions: The caterpillar might have found all of his foods in a refrigerator. Draw some of the foods that are in your refrigerator at home.

Vocabulary Overview

Key words and phrases from this section are provided below with definitions and sentences about how the words are used in the story. Introduce and discuss these important vocabulary words with the students. If you think these words or other words in the story warrant more time devoted to them, there are suggestions in the introduction for other vocabulary activities (page 5).

Word	Definition	Sentence about Text
emerge	come into view	A butterfly **emerges** from its cocoon.
beautiful	pleasing to see	The butterfly is covered with **beautiful** colors.
butterfly	an insect with a slender body, antennae and colorful wings	The story is about a caterpillar that changes into a **butterfly.**
fly	move through the air	After he emerges, the butterfly learns to **fly**.
soar	ride on the wind high in the air	The happy butterfly **soars** through the air.
predict	say what you think will happen in the future	It is fun to **predict** what might happen to the butterfly.
dream	a hope or a desire	What might the butterfly **dream** of doing when he flies away?
future	a time that has not yet happened	What will the caterpillar do in the **future**?
life cycle	a series of changes passed through by living things	We learn about the **life cycle** of a butterfly in this story.

Name _____

Vocabulary Activity

Directions: Write at least two sentences using words from the story.

Words from the Story

emerge	beautiful	butterfly	fly
predict	dream	future	life cycle

_____

- - - - - - - - - - - - - - - - - -

_____

_____

- - - - - - - - - - - - - - - - - -

_____

_____

_____

_____

Directions: Answer this question.

1. What do you **predict** will happen to the **beautiful butterfly**?

_____

- - - - - - - - - - - - - - - - - -

_____

_____

Analyzing the Literature

Provided below are discussion questions you can use in small groups, with the whole class, or for written assignments. Each question is written at two levels so you can choose the right question for each group of students. For each question, a few key points are provided for your reference as you discuss the book with the students.

Story Element	Level 1	Level 2	Key Discussion Points
Character	What is the caterpillar thinking about when he hatches from the egg?	What do you think the caterpillar imagines when he thinks about his future?	There is no way of knowing whether or not a caterpillar realizes that someday he will be a butterfly. Obviously meeting the immediate hunger need is of primary concern to the caterpillar. Allow students to speculate on what dreams the caterpillar might have.
Character	What makes the butterfly beautiful?	What things are beautiful about the egg and the caterpillar?	The butterfly is beautifully colored. There is beauty in an egg's simplicity and promise of new life. Some students might consider the caterpillar cute and maybe even beautiful.
Setting	Where are some places the butterfly might fly?	If you were able to fly like a butterfly, where would you like to visit?	There are many places a butterfly might go. He may visit the place he was born or places to get more food. He may also want to fly off and explore the world.
Plot	What will happen next to the butterfly?	If you were to write a story about the butterfly, where would it take place?	Children are free to use their imaginations to create stories about what will happen next to the butterfly. Will the butterfly continue to be as hungry as he was as a caterpillar?

Name _____

Reader Response

Think

Think about where you would fly if you had wings. Why would you choose that location?

Narrative Writing Prompt

Write a story that tells where you would fly if you had wings. Be sure you describe the location using adjectives.

_____

- -

_____

- -

_____

- -

_____

- -

_____

- -

_____

- -

_____

Name _____

Making Connections—My Prediction for the Future

Directions: Find a partner. Talk about these questions for a few minutes. Then, think about your answers and fill in the speech bubbles below.

- What activities will you enjoy when you are older?
- What type of job would you like to have?
- What do you think your family will be like?

Name _____

Making connections—Giving Advice

Directions: Imagine that an adult butterfly comes to visit the tiny caterpillar at the beginning of the book.

1. Draw a picture of a butterfly and a tiny caterpillar.

2. Make a speech bubble for each character.

3. Write the butterfly's advice for the caterpillar in his speech bubble.

4. Write a question the caterpillar may have for the butterfly in the caterpillar's speech bubble.

Name _____

Language Learning—Exclamations!

Directions: Write at least three sentences about the butterfly. Each one must end with an exclamation point.

_____

_____

_____

_____

_____

_____

_____

_____

_____

_____

_____

_____

_____

Name _____

Story Elements—Characters

This book shows how a caterpillar grows and changes through his life. Think of ways you have grown and changed. Draw pictures showing what you could do as a baby, what you could do when you were two or three, and what you can do now. Share your pictures with a friend and explain how you have changed.

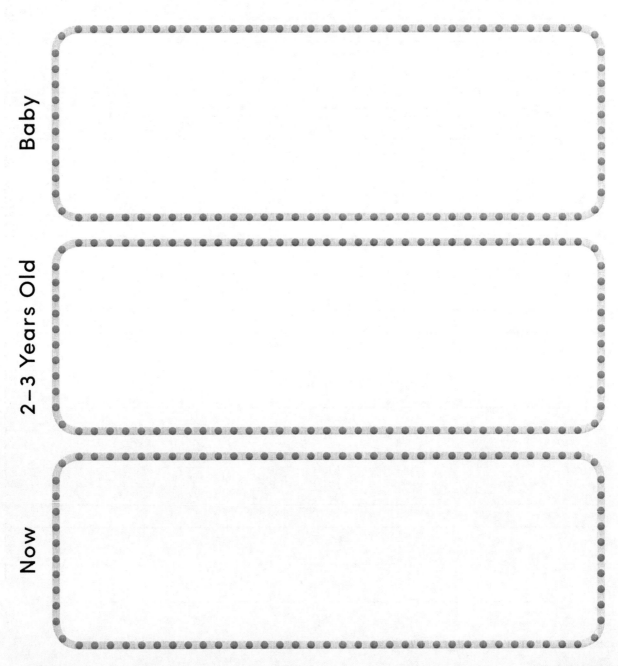

Baby

2–3 Years Old

Now

Name _____

Story Elements—Setting

Directions: How would this story be different if the setting were in your school cafeteria? Make a diagram that shows where the caterpillar will go and what the caterpillar will eat in your school.

#40008—Instructional Guide: The Very Hungry Caterpillar

Name _____

Post-Reading Theme Thoughts

Directions: Choose the small caterpillar, big caterpillar, or butterfly from *The Very Hungry Caterpillar*. Pretend you are that character. Draw a picture of a happy face or a sad face to show how the character would feel about each statement below. Then use words to explain your picture.

Character I Chose _____

Statement	How Does He Feel? 😊 ☹	Explain How the Character Feels
A character can change a lot between the beginning of a story and the end.		
A caterpillar stays very busy.		
It is important to make good food choices.		
It takes a lot of work to become a butterfly.		

#40008—Instructional Guide: The Very Hungry Caterpillar

Culminating Activity:
Create a Caterpillar's Excursion

Directions: Allow students to form small groups and select one of the following activities. Most likely, these activities will require some adult assistance to complete. The pictures on pages 62–64 may be fun for students to use as they create their performances.

Retell the Caterpillar's Excursion—Review the story of *The Very Hungry Caterpillar.* Cut apart the pictures on pages 62–64 to help retell the story in the correct order. Retell the story in your own words.

Create a New Excursion for the Caterpillar—Think of a new adventure the caterpillar could have. Where would he go? What would he do? What would he eat? Write your new story and cut apart the pictures on pages 62–64 or create props to tell your story.

An Excursion for a Butterfly—The caterpillar has transformed into a butterfly. The butterfly is off to see the world. Write a reader's theater script about the adventures the butterfly has. Create puppets and props to go along with your drama.

culminating Activity: create a caterpillar's excursion (cont.)

Directions: Reproduce the patterns on tagboard or construction paper. Have the students cut them apart. To create stick puppets, glue each pattern to a tongue depressor or craft stick.

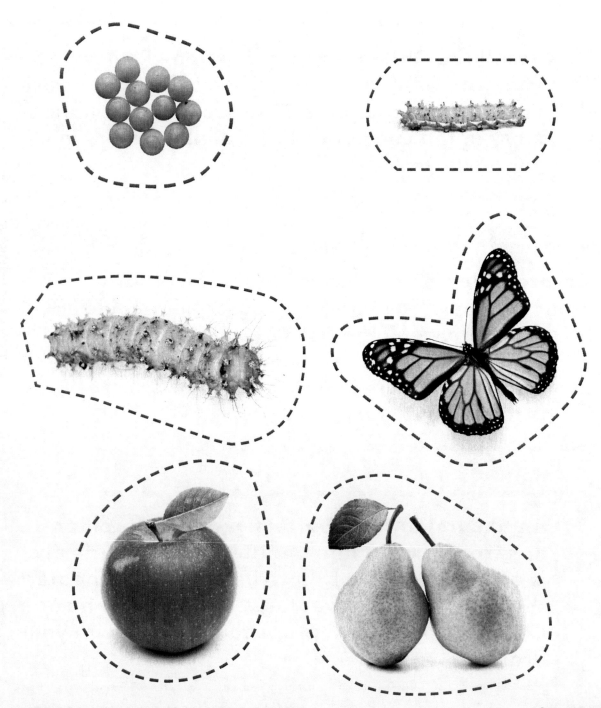

culminating Activity: create a caterpillar's Excursion (cont.)

Culminating Activity: Create a Caterpillar's Excursion (cont.)

Name _____

comprehension Assessment

Directions: Fill in the bubble for the best response to each question.

1. Which sentence best describes the caterpillar at the beginning of the story?

(A) The caterpillar is huge.

(B) He is sleeping on a leaf.

(C) He is hungry and very small.

(D) The caterpillar's stomach hurts.

2. Show how the caterpillar changes by writing these words in the correct order.

cocoon	big caterpillar	egg	butterfly	tiny caterpillar

_____

_____

_____

_____

_____

_____

_____

_____

comprehension Assessment (cont.)

3. What describes how the caterpillar feels on Saturday?

   (A) He is tired and needs a nap.

   (B) He is hungry.

   (C) He grows from small to large.

   (D) He is changing inside his cocoon.

4. Give examples of how the caterpillar makes both good and poor food choices in this story.

   _____

   -

   _____

   -

   _____

   -

   _____

5. What is one thing the caterpillar does before he gets a stomachache?

   (A) He makes a cocoon.

   (B) He eats a nice leaf.

   (C) He turns into a beautiful butterfly.

   (D) He starts to look for some food.

Name _____

Response to Literature: The Best Part of a Butterfly

Directions: Complete the following steps. Then, answer the questions on the next page.

1. Think about the parts of a butterfly's life.

2. Circle your favorite part of a butterfly's life.

egg   **tiny caterpillar**   **big caterpillar**

cocoon   **butterfly**

3. Draw a picture of when you like the caterpillar/ butterfly best. Make sure your picture shows what he is doing. Your drawing should be bold, detailed, and colorful.

Name _____

Response to Literature: The Best Part of a Butterfly (cont.)

1. What do you think is the best part of a butterfly's life?

_____

- - - - - - - - - - - - - - - -

_____
_____

- - - - - - - - - - - - - - - -

_____

2. Why do you think this is the best part of his life?

_____

- - - - - - - - - - - - - - - -

_____
_____

- - - - - - - - - - - - - - - -

_____

3. What will happen next to the caterpillar/butterfly in your drawing?

_____

- - - - - - - - - - - - - - - -

_____
_____

- - - - - - - - - - - - - - - -

Name _____

Response to Literature Rubric

Directions: Use this rubric to evaluate student responses.

Great Job	Good Work	Keep Trying
☐ You answered all three questions completely. You included many details.	☐ You answered all three questions.	☐ You did not answer all three questions.
☐ Your handwriting is very neat. There are no spelling errors.	☐ Your handwriting can be neater. There are some spelling errors.	☐ Your handwriting is not very neat. There are many spelling errors.
☐ Your picture is neat and fully colored.	☐ Your picture is neat and some of it is colored.	☐ Your picture is not very neat and/or fully colored.
☐ Creativity is clear in both the picture and the writing.	☐ Creativity is clear in either the picture or the writing.	☐ There is not much creativity in either the picture or the writing.

Teacher Comments: _____

_____

_____

_____

Name _____

_____

- -

_____

_____

- -

_____

_____

- -

_____

_____

- -

_____

The responses provided here are just examples of what the students may answer. Many accurate responses are possible for the questions throughout this unit.

Vocabulary Activity—Section 1:
Meet the Caterpillar (page 16)
1. Many things can be described as **beautiful**. This might be a good time to introduce the concept that beauty is in the eye of the beholder and that if one looks carefully, they can see beauty in most anything.

Guided Close Reading—Section 1:
Meet the Caterpillar (page 19)
1. The egg is described as being little. Synonyms for little include: small, tiny, teeny, and not big.
2. The caterpillar is described as being tiny and very hungry. The caterpillar could also be described as small, green and yellow, short, or thin.
3. The book starts with a calm and peaceful night scene. The caterpillar hatches on a bright, beautiful, sunny day.

Vocabulary Activity—Section 2:
Watch the Caterpillar Change (page 25)
- The small egg **hatches** when it's ready.
- In the moonlight a small **egg** is on a leaf.
- The caterpillar hatches from an **egg**.
- The caterpillar builds a small house called a **cocoon**.
- When he emerges from the cocoon, he is a beautiful **butterfly**!
1. **Caterpillar** is another name for **larva**.

Guided Close Reading—Section 2:
Watch the Caterpillar Change (page 28)
1. After eating Monday through Friday, the caterpillar is still hungry. The caterpillar eats a feast on Saturday and has a stomachache that night. On Sunday the caterpillar is no longer hungry or little; he is big and fat.
2. A cocoon is a small house for the caterpillar. The butterfly is able to come out of the cocoon by nibbling a small hole.
3. The book states that the caterpillar stays in the cocoon for more than two weeks.

Making Connections—Section 2:
Watch the Caterpillar Change (page 29)
1. egg
2. caterpillar
3. cocoon
4. butterfly

Language Learning—Section 2:
Watch the Caterpillar Change (page 30)
- Check students' sentences to make sure they include capital letters and end punctuation.

Vocabulary Activity—Section 3:
Math Concepts with the Caterpillar (page 34)
- He starts to look for food.
- He eats through three plums.
- On Saturday he eats through one piece of chocolate cake.
- He eats through one slice of salami.
- The next day is Sunday again.
- He eats through a leaf and feels better.

Guided Close Reading—Section 3:
Math Concepts with the Caterpillar (page 37)
1. The amount of food the caterpillar eats increases each day of the week. Finally on Saturday he eats a feast.
2. On Monday through Friday, the caterpillar eats more and more fruit. On Saturday the caterpillar eats through ten pieces of food (chocolate cake, ice-cream cone, a pickle, Swiss cheese, a salami, a lollipop, cherry pie, sausage, a cupcake, and a watermelon).
3. During the week, "He was still hungry" is used to tell how he is feeling. On Saturday the caterpillar gets a stomachache from all the food he eats throughout the day.

Making Connections—Section 3:
Math Concepts with the Caterpillar (page 38)

Day of the Week	Fruit the Caterpillar Eats	How Many Pieces
Monday		1
Tuesday		2
Wednesday		3
Thursday		4
Friday		5
Total Pieces of Fruit the Caterpillar Eats:		15

Language Learning—Section 3:
Math Concepts with the Caterpillar (page 39)
1. Caterpillars eat apples
2. The caterpillar likes to eat fruit.
3. Caterpillars turn into butterflies.

Vocabulary Activity—Section 4:
What Should the Caterpillar Eat? (page 43)
1. On Sunday he eats through a **slice** of Swiss cheese.
2. The caterpillar eats through three **plums**.
3. He also eats through a piece of **cherry pie**.
4. The caterpillar also eats **through** an apple, pears, strawberries, oranges, chocolate cake, an ice-cream cone, a pickle, a slice of salami, a lollipop, a sausage, a cupcake, a slice of watermelon, and a leaf.

Guided Close Reading—Section 4:
What Should the Caterpillar Eat? (page 46)
1. The story lists all the foods the caterpillar eats on Saturday and then says, "That night he had a stomachache!"
2. The text names and pictures show ten different foods the caterpillar eats on Saturday.
3. The caterpillar eats through one green leaf to feel better.

Making Connections—Section 4:
What Should the Caterpillar Eat? (page 47)
The pictures should be sorted into the following groups:

Fruit/Vegetable	Meat (Protein)
apple, pear, plum, strawberry, orange, and watermelon	slice of salami and sausage
Dairy	**Empty Calories**
slice of Swiss cheese	chocolate cake, ice-cream cone, pickle, lollipop, cherry pie, and cupcake

Language Learning—Section 4:
What Should the Caterpillar Eat? (page 48)
1. apple
2. ice-cream cone
3. leaf
4. oranges
5. strawberries
6. watermelon

Vocabulary Activity—Section 5:
What Will Happen to the Caterpillar? (page 52)
1. Any reasonable predictions of what may happen to the beautiful butterfly are acceptable. Try to help children see that the butterfly will most likely continue the life cycle and soon there will be another egg lying on a leaf waiting to hatch.

Comprehension Assessment (pages 65–66)
1. C. He is hungry and very small.
2. egg, tiny caterpillar, big caterpillar, cocoon, butterfly
3. B. He is hungry.
4. The caterpillar makes good food choices at first. He chooses fruit. On Saturday he makes very poor food decisions by eating through cake, ice cream, a lollipop, pie, and a cupcake. He also eats a large quantity of food Saturday which was another reason he did not feel well that night.
5. D. He starts to look for some food.